SUPER-EASY
STEP-BY-STEP
WINEMAKING

Other Books by Yvonne Young Tarr
The Ten Minute Gourmet Cookbook
The Ten Minute Gourmet Diet Cookbook
101 Desserts to Make You Famous
Love Portions
The New York Times Natural Foods Kieting Book
The Complete Outdoor Cookbook
The New York Times Bread and Soup Cookbook
The Farmhouse Cookbook
Super-Easy Step-by-Step Cheesemaking
Super-Easy Step-by-Step Sausagemaking
Super-Easy Step-by-Step Book of Special Breads
The Up-with-Wholesome, Down-with-Storebought
Book of Recipes and Household Formulas

SUPER-EASY STEP-BY-STEP WINEMAKING

YVONNE YOUNG TARR

Vintage Books
A Division of Random House, Inc.
New York

VINTAGE BOOKS EDITION 1975
FIRST EDITION

Copyright © 1975 by Yvonne Young Tarr

All rights reserved under International and
Pan-American Copyright Conventions.
Published in the United States by Random
House, Inc., New York, and simultaneously
in Canada by Random House of Canada
Limited, Toronto.

Library of Congress Cataloging in Publication Data

Tarr, Yvonne Young.
Super-easy step-by-step Winemaking
1. Wine and wine making—Amateurs' manuals.
I. Title.
TP548.2.T37 1975 641.8'72 75-13620
ISBN 0-394-72012-1

Manufactured in the United States of America

INTRODUCTION

Winemaking is not an art—it is child's play. Nearly every fruit, many flowers and even some vegetables magically transform themselves into wine when they are mixed with sugar, water and yeast and allowed to ferment until they clear. The trick is *not merely to produce wine but to produce FINE wine.* To do this you must either have experience in making wine or *an accurate recipe* written by a winemaker with years of experience.

This is the book with the recipes that really work. A modern book using modern methods, accurate ingredients and non-metric measurements, it bears no relationship to other wine-making books that are often imprecise and outdated—hodge-podges of recipes and directions written in terms you cannot understand, using ingredients not available in America.

This book takes you by the hand and leads you step-by-step through super-easy directions. Each process is so clearly and so directly explained that it is virtually impossible to make a mistake.

Don't let the looks of the equipment or the complex-sounding names frighten you away. Explanations of procedures, equipment and terms are given in easy-to-understand paragraphs on pages 1 to 9 and 79 to 107. Don't read these first and confuse yourself unnecessarily. When you are actually in the process of making your first wine, you will suddenly understand everything.

If you enjoy trying something new, love fine wines and would like to make them for just pennies a bottle, DO try the wonderful experience of making your own wines.

IMPORTANT NOTE

Federal laws regulating the production of alcoholic beverages in the home are quite liberal. Heads of household may, upon filing duplicate copies of registration form 1541 with the Internal Revenue Service, make up to 200 tax-free gallons of wine per year for household consumption.

Obtain form 1541 by writing to the office of the Assistant Regional Commissioner, Alcohol and Tobacco Tax, in the district nearest your home. Winemaking may begin as soon as the forms are filed.

WHY MAKE FRUIT AND FLOWER WINES?

When most enthusiasts think of wine they think of grape wine, either white or red. In fact, there are dozens of splendid wines that use not a single grape. This book gives recipes for only two wines from fresh grapes and many more for other, more fascinating varieties. Why? First, because fresh grapes are often outrageously expensive, even in season, and wines made from them can cost as much as two dollars per bottle. Second, because really fine grape wines are tricky to make, generally requiring an accurate blending of two or more varieties of grapes to produce mellow wines consistently high in quality. Third, because red wines from fresh grapes should be aged for at least a year in the bottle, and few winemakers (especially beginners) have the patience to wait them out.

Flower wines and fruit wines from canned fruits, on the other hand, cost pennies per bottle to make, behave predictably and are generally ready to drink in half the time it takes grape wines to mature. Once you brew a few of these more ethereal wines, you may consider, as I do, that grape wines are difficult, even a bit boring, and most often not worth the additional time and money.

Contents

THE WINEMAKING PROCESS SIMPLIFIED AND SPECIAL INGREDIENTS

WINEMAKING SIMPLIFIED

The winemaking process consists of the following steps:
1. ... Making a must by mixing the basic ingredients as indicated in the wine recipe you choose
2. ... Allowing the must to ferment (Primary Fermentation)
3. ... Siphoning the must into a clean jug, leaving the heavy sediment behind (First Racking)
4. ... Filling the jug to the top and sealing it with an air lock (Topping Off)
5. ... Allowing this young wine to ferment until it is fairly clear (Secondary Fermentation)
6. ... Siphoning the partially cleared wine into a clean jug (Second Racking and Third Racking)
7. ... Topping off the jug and fitting it with an air lock each time
8. ... Allowing the wine to clear completely in the jug
9. ... Doing a Candle Test to make certain the wine is clear enough to be bottled
10. ... Bottling the wine and sealing with corks or caps
11. ... Aging the wine until it is mellow enough to drink

SPECIAL INGREDIENTS FOR WINEMAKING

The ingredients listed below are inexpensive and readily available in wine supply and other stores (*see* Sources of Supply, page 107).
While good wines can be made at home without these special ingredients (simply by adding sugar and lemons until the must reaches the tart sweetness of well-flavored lemonade), your homemade wines will be far superior if you do include these, plus a good wine yeast, in your recipes.

CRYSTALS: (sodium or potassium metabisulfite, food grade), for sterilizing equipment and musts.

WINE YEAST: Only a true wine yeast will insure the even fermentation and firm yeast deposit which makes the must and finished wine easier to rack. Wine yeasts usually come in small foil envelopes for convenience in storing and using. Buy the self-starting variety, since these may be added directly to the must without the mess and fuss of making a starter solution. Don't use baker's or brewer's yeast, which may produce bitterness and off-flavors in wines.

YEAST NUTRIENT: A blend of ammonium salts used to nourish the yeast and help it work actively.

ACID BLEND *(BLENDS OF MIXED ACIDS)*: Or separate packets of *tartaric, citric* and *malic acids* for mixing your own blend (2 parts tartaric and 2 parts citric to 1 part malic).

GRAPE TANNIN: To add to the flavor of all wines.

PECTIC ENZYMES: To remove wine-clouding excess pectin from pectin-laden stone fruits such as peaches, nectarines, etc.

EQUIPMENT

BASIC EQUIPMENT

The first rule in winemaking is "never buy what you can scrounge." You can find, borrow or salvage many pieces of necessary equipment from the refuse bin in your own kitchen. One-gallon cider jugs make perfect secondary fermentation vessels, a clean nylon stocking is the best strainer going, and wine bottles are generally available for free from friends or friendly restaurant owners.

Plastic, glass, wood, stainless steel or unchipped enamelware are the only materials in which fine wines should be made. Avoid any metal other than stainless steel. Metal contamination is absolutely impossible to remedy, and wines thus afflicted will have to be destroyed.

BASIC EQUIPMENT FOR PRIMARY FERMENTATION

PRIMARY FERMENTOR: To make 1 gallon of wine you will need a 3-gallon plastic container. A new plastic wastebasket will do nicely.

To make 5 gallons of wine, a new 8-gallon plastic garbage can is ideal. Don't worry if it doesn't come with a cover, for you'll be using plastic sheeting tied down with string or a large rubber band. The plastic that covers your dry cleaning is perfect for this purpose.

LONG-HANDLED WOODEN SPOONS: For stirring ingredients. Be sure these are long enough to keep your hand above the liquid level.

PLASTIC MEASURING SPOONS AND PLASTIC OR GLASS MEASURING CUP: For measuring ingredients.

PLASTIC GRAVY BASTER: For withdrawing wine samples when measuring sugar content.

PLASTIC FUNNELS

LONG-HANDLED NYLON BRUSHES: For scrubbing containers and jars.

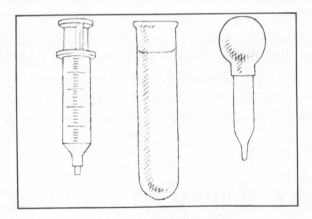

ACID TITRATION KIT *(OPTIONAL)*: For measuring the total acid content of your wine. While the recipes in this book are designed to produce good wines, the acid content of fruit (like its sugar content) varies, depending on soil and climate conditions during the growing period. Titrating or testing for total acids assures that your wine will have perfect acid balance. (*See* Acid Control, page 85.)

A FLOATING WINE THERMOMETER: To make sure the must is at the correct temperature before adding the yeast. A new plastic fishtank thermometer is ideal.

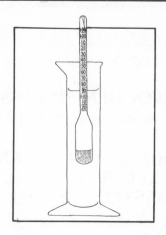

HYDROMETER OR SACCHAROMETER AND HYDRO-METER JAR *(OPTIONAL)*: For measuring the sugar content of your primary fermentation. (*See* Sugar Control, page 82.)

CRUSHERS AND PRESSES: Crushers and presses are unnecessary unless you plan to make wine in batches of more than 30 gallons. Otherwise, a small wooden masher, a mortar and pestle or a good electric blender will work perfectly.

A STRONG NYLON BAG OR CLEAN NYLON STOCK-ING: To help you strain and squeeze juices from your crushed fruit.

BASIC EQUIPMENT FOR RACKING

SECONDARY FERMENTOR: One- or 2-gallon narrow-necked glass jug or jar, or the larger 5-gallon jar (carboy), to hold the wine after primary fermentation is finished. The size jug you need depends on whether you're making 1, 2 or 5 gallons of wine.

PLASTIC OR RUBBER SIPHON HOSE: To siphon wine from one vessel to another. You will need a 5-foot piece of tubing with an inside diameter of at least ⅜-inch. See-through plastic tubing is best, but surgical tubing from your drugstore will do.

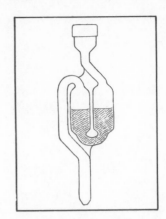

AIR LOCK: Also called fermentation lock or trap. This glass or rigid plastic device comes complete with stopper or bung. Partially filled with metabisulfite sterile solution, it fits the narrow neck of the jug and prevents air from contaminating your wine while simultaneously allowing fermentation gases to escape.

BASIC EQUIPMENT FOR BOTTLING

WINE BOTTLES: Use standard wine bottles of pint or fifth capacity. Only these are designed to receive long, straight wine corks. Their uniform size also makes them easy to store. You may buy these new, or scrounge them from friends or restaurants. Whether new or previously used, dark-green or brown bottles are best for red wines, while white wines may go into light-green or even clear bottles. For your fruit wines other than grape you may prefer bottles with screw tops, but in any case, avoid odd-shaped bottles or those with threads that are not standard. Closures may not be available for these.

CLOSURES: Use only brand-new, straight-sided (not tapered) wine corks or plastic screw tops. Ordinary household corks are not suitable.

A CORKING DEVICE: A handy device to drive corks deep into the necks of bottles. This may be a hand-held or table-mounted machine.

RECIPES

DANDELION WINE

Dandelion wine has a bitey, slightly bitter aftertaste reminiscent of fresh flowers nibbled on a bright spring day. It is clear and pale yellow and surprisingly dry. You won't find its like on any liquor-store shelf.

(Yield: 2 gallons)

STEP ONE
PRIMARY FERMENTATION

INGREDIENTS

3 Quarts fully opened dandelion flowers
1 Gallon very hot water
3½ Cups sugar
2 Oranges
2 Lemons
1 Teaspoon grape tannin
5½ Teaspoons acid blend
1 Teaspoon yeast nutrient
1 Campden tablet
1 Package self-starting all-purpose wine yeast

EQUIPMENT

Large plastic funnel or nylon strainer
Cheesecloth
In addition to these two items you will need the equipment listed on pages 6 to 8.

A. You will need about 3 quarts of fully opened, perfect blossoms with no stems or leaves attached. Pick flowerheads that have not begun to go to seed, from a field or lawn uncontaminated by weedkillers, tree sprays or exhaust fumes. Pack a pic-nic lunch to eat during a break from blossom-gathering and next year bring a bottle of your own delicious dandelion wine!

B. Discard any insects (although they probably won't dam-age the wine) and place your flowers in a clean plastic contain-er. Rinse lightly with cold water, drain well and cover with one gallon of hot, not boiling, water. Stir to moisten all flowers. Cover the container with plastic sheeting and tie down tightly. Allow the dandelion heads to steep for 5 days, stirring once daily. Re-tie the plastic cover each time. The odor may not be too pleasant, but the flavor will be there.

STEP TWO
ON THE FIFTH DAY . . .

A. Set out and sterilize your equipment (*see* How to Sterilize with Metabisulfites, page 80).

B. Line a large plastic funnel or nylon strainer with cheese-cloth to catch the flowerheads as you pour the liquid into your primary container. Gather the soggy blossoms in the cheese-cloth and squeeze out as much liquid as possible. Discard cheesecloth and flowers.

C. Measure 2 cups of the strained liquid into a glass pot or stainless-steel saucepan. Add 3½ cups of sugar, bring to a boil, and stir with a wooden spoon until sugar is dissolved. Cool syrup for 5 minutes, then add to liquid in the primary container. Cut the thin orange or yellow outer skin from the oranges and lemons (include none of the bitter white underskin). Cut the lemons and oranges into sections, discard the seeds and squeeze the juice into the dandelion must. Drop in the squeezed-out fruit as well. Stir the grape tannin, acid blend and yeast nutrient in thoroughly. Crush and add the Campden tablet.

D. While the must cools, withdraw a sample with your baster and test for sugar content (*see* Sugar Control, page 82). Specific gravity should be 1.088 or Balling 22.0. Titrate another sample for acid content (*see* Acid Control, page 85.) Acid content should be .60 percent. Adjust for sugar or acid if necessary, as explained on page 107.

E. Take the temperature of your wine, and when it registers between 72 and 78 degrees F. set the primary container with the must in the place where it will undergo primary fermentation.

F. Sprinkle the yeast over the top of the must but do *not* stir in. Tie the plastic sheeting over the container, allow the yeast to work for 12 hours, then remove the covering and stir the yeast in well. Re-cover and tie down.

STEP THREE
DAILY CHECKS

Allow the must to ferment for 5 days, stirring daily, *or* until the specific gravity drops to 1.030 or the Balling scale registers 8.0.

If the specific gravity falls below the ideal level, proceed with the first racking anyway. The wine is still good.

STEP FOUR
FIRST RACKING

INGREDIENTS
3½ Cups sugar
1 Quart water

EQUIPMENT
2 1-gallon glass jugs or jars
Siphon hose
2 Air locks

A. Rinse 2 1-gallon glass jugs with stock sterile solution and prepare 2 air locks (see How to Sterilize with Metabisulfites, page 80).

B. Rack the must into the jugs in equal amounts, leaving the yeasty sediment behind (see How to Rack Wines, First Racking, page 87).

C. Place 3½ cups of sugar in a glass or stainless-steel pot, add 1 quart of water and bring to a boil. Remove from heat and stir until sugar is dissolved. Cool the syrup and use it to top off, adding half to each gallon of must (see Topping Off, page 91).

D. Seal each gallon with an air lock (see How to Fit an Air Lock, page 93). Allow the wine to ferment for 3 weeks undisturbed and then proceed with second racking.

STEP FIVE
SECOND RACKING

INGREDIENTS
½ Cup sugar
1⅓ Cups boiling water
1 Campden tablet

EQUIPMENT
2 1-gallon glass jugs or jars
Siphon hose
2 Air locks

A. Sterilize equipment with metabisulfites (*see* page 80).

B. Rack each gallon into a sterile glass jug (*see* Second Racking, page 89).

C. Prepare a sugar syrup with ½ cup of sugar dissolved in 1⅓ cups of boiling water. Cool the syrup, crush the Campden tablet into it, and top off the 2 gallons (*see* page 91).

D. Attach air locks and fill with fresh sterile solution (*see* page 93).

E. Store, undisturbed, in a cool dark place for 3 months, by which time the wine should be quite clear and pale yellow in color.

STEP SIX
THIRD RACKING

INGREDIENTS
1 Campden tablet
2 Cups water

EQUIPMENT
2 1-gallon glass jugs or jars
Siphon hose
2 Air locks

A. Sterilize 2 gallon jugs and 2 air locks in stock sulfite solution (*see* page 80).

B. Crush 1 Campden tablet in 2 cups of tap water. Pour half of this solution into each of the clean jugs.

C. Rack the wine into the jugs containing the metabisulfite solution, taking great care to include *none* of the sediment and to aerate the wine as little as possible (*see* Third Racking, page 89).

D. Top off with tepid tap water (*see* page 91).

E. Sterilize the air locks and immediately place them on the jugs of wine (*see* page 93).

F. Allow to remain undisturbed in a cool, dark place until perfectly clear (about 6 to 9 months).

STEP SEVEN
CANDLE TEST

When the wine seems perfectly clear, use the Candle Test (*see* page 95) to determine whether it is ready to bottle. If there is any cloudiness, replace stale sulfite solution with fresh and set jugs aside for 2 more months. Do another Candle Test at the end of this time. If the wine meets all requirements, it is ready to bottle.

STEP EIGHT
BOTTLING THE WINE

EQUIPMENT
10 25-ounce wine bottles or 9 25-ounce
bottles and 2 half-bottles
Siphon hose
Appropriate closures

A. If the Candle Test indicates no signs of active fermentation, your wine is ready to bottle (*see* How to Bottle Wines, page 99).

B. Remember that cleanliness is vital and that overexposure to air at this point could cause the wine to expire.

C. Taste the wine. If it is fairly mellow, age it only a few months before sampling a small bottle. You will probably be able to judge from this first bottle how much longer, if at all, your wine needs to age.

VIOLET WINE

Despite their fragile appearance, the lovely blue-purple blossoms of the not-so-common violet impart a delicately light, lingering flavor and an excellent bouquet when made into wine.
(Yield: 1 gallon)

STEP ONE
PRIMARY FERMENTATION

INGREDIENTS
4 Quarts violets
10 Cups hot water
1¾ Cups sugar
1 Cup boiling water
4 Oranges, peeled
3 Lemons, peeled
2 Teaspoons acid blend
¾ Teaspoon grape tannin
½ Campden tablet
½ Teaspoon yeast nutrient
1 Package self-starting all-purpose wine yeast

EQUIPMENT
Large plastic funnel or nylon strainer
Cheesecloth
Plus Basic Equipment for Primary
Fermentation as outlined on page 6.

A. Pick only the flowers, leaving behind stalks, leaves and any resident insects. When you have collected 4 quarts, place the petals in a plastic primary container and cover with 10 cups of hot water. Tie plastic over container top, and allow flowers to steep for 3 days to transfer their subtle color and delicate bouquet to the must.

STEP TWO
ON THE FOURTH DAY...

A. Rinse equipment with stock metabisulfite solution (*see* How to Sterilize with Metabisulfites, page 80).

B. Line funnel or strainer with cheesecloth. Pour the violet must through the cheesecloth into the primary container. Gather the corners of the cheesecloth and wring out any remaining liquid. Discard the violets.

C. Dissolve 1¾ cups of sugar in 1 cup of boiling water. Cool to room temperature. Stir cooled syrup into the violet must.

D. Discard the skin of the oranges and lemons (including the bitter white underskin) and cut fruit in half. Squeeze the juice from fruit into the must as you add each piece.

E. Crush the Campden tablet, mix with a little water and stir into the must. Stir in all other ingredients except the yeast.

F. Withdraw a sample of the must with your baster and test for sugar content (*see* Sugar Control, page 82). Specific gravity should be 1.084 or Balling 21.0. Test for total acids (see Acid Control, page 85). Acid content should be .60 percent. Add more sugar or acid blend if necessary, rechecking after each addition.

G. When the must temperature registers between 72 and 78 degrees F., transfer the primary container to the place where it will undergo its primary fermentation and sprinkle the yeast over the top of the must. Tie plastic over container top. Allow yeast to work for 12 hours, then stir in thoroughly with a long-handled spoon. Re-cover container with plastic sheet and tie down tightly. Stir daily for 6 days, re-covering securely each time.

STEP THREE
DAILY CHECKS

After you stir the must on the third day, check the progress of the fermentation with your hydrometer or saccharometer (see Sugar Control, page 82). Do this each day hereafter until the specific gravity drops to 1.023 (Balling: 6). The must is then ready to be transferred to a gallon jug for its secondary fermentation. (If the specific gravity falls below 1.023 (Balling: 6) rack anyway. The wine is still good.)

STEP FOUR
FIRST RACKING

INGREDIENTS
½ Cup sugar
¼ Cup boiling water

EQUIPMENT
1-gallon glass jug or jar
Siphon hose
Air lock

A. Rinse a 1-gallon glass jug with stock sterile solution and prepare an air lock (sse How to Sterilize with Metabisulfites, page 80).

B. Rack must into gallon jar (see How to Rack Wines, First Racking, page 87).

C. Top off (see Topping Off, page 91) with cooled sugar syrup prepared by dissolving ½ cup of sugar in ¼ cup of boiling water.

D. Seal jar with air lock, allow to ferment undisturbed for 3 weeks, and then proceed with second racking.

STEP FIVE
SECOND RACKING

INGREDIENTS
¼ Cup sugar
⅔ Cup boiling water

EQUIPMENT
1-gallon glass jug or jar
Siphon hose
Air lock

A. Sterilize equipment with metabisulfite (*see* page 80).

B. Rack again (*see* Second Racking, page 89).

C. Top off with sugar syrup made by dissolving ¼ cup of sugar in ⅔ cup boiling water (*see* Topping Off, page 91). Cool the syrup before adding to the must.

D. Seal with an air lock filled with fresh metabisulfite solution.

E. Set the container in a cool, dark place to ferment for 3 months.

STEP SIX
THIRD RACKING

INGREDIENTS
½ Campden tablet
1 Cup water

EQUIPMENT
1-gallon glass jug or jar
Air lock
Siphon hose

A. Sterilize a 1-gallon glass jug, air lock and hose (*see* page 80).

B. Rack the wine (*see* How to Rack Wines, Third Racking, page 89).

C. Top off with ½ crushed Campden tablet mixed with 1 cup or sufficient tepid water to fill jug (*see* page 91).

D. Fit sterile air lock in place (*see* page 93).

E. Allow to remain undisturbed in a cool, dark place until clear (about 6 to 9 months).

STEP SEVEN
CANDLE TEST

A. When the wine seems perfectly clear, use Candle Test to determine whether it is ready to bottle (*see* page 95). If there is any cloudiness, replace air lock with fresh sulfite solution, set aside for 2 more months, then re-test. When wine passes Candle Test, proceed with bottling.

STEP EIGHT
BOTTLING THE WINE

EQUIPMENT
5 25-ounce wine bottles or
4 25-ounce wine bottles and 2 half-bottles
Siphon hose
Appropriate closures

A. Instructions for bottling are given in the How to Bottle Wines section (*see* page 99).

STEP NINE
STORING AND AGING THE WINE

A. General instructions for storing and aging your wine appear on page 101.

B. Violet Wine matures rapidly and may be sampled 4 to 6 months after bottling. If the wine still tastes a little raw, age the remaining bottles for 2 to 3 months, then sample again.

ROSE-PETAL WINE

Fragrant rose petals make a lovely wine with a fragile pink color and a delicate bouquet.

(Yield: 1 gallon)

STEP ONE
PRIMARY FERMENTATION

INGREDIENTS

3 Quarts rose petals
2½ Quarts boiling water
½ Campden tablet
½ 100-milligram ascorbic acid tablet
3½ Cups sugar
1½ Cups water
2 Cups freshly-squeezed orange juice
4 Teaspoons acid blend
1 Teaspoon yeast nutrient
1 Package self-starting all-purpose wine
yeast

EQUIPMENT

An extra primary container
Large plastic funnel or nylon strainer
Cheesecloth
Equipment as listed in Basic Equipment for
Primary Fermentation, *see* page 6

A. At the height of their bloom, gather roses that have never been sprayed or exposed to the pollution of passing cars. Never use roses from a florist; most of these have been sprayed.

B. Pull off petals. Discard centers and stems. The insects inhabiting your roses will probably have vanished by the time they reach your kitchen, but examine the petals anyway for any stubborn aphids. Unless the petals are mud-spattered by recent rains, there is no need to rinse them.

C. Place petals in a primary container and cover with 2½ quarts of boiling water. Crush ½ Campden tablet and ½ ascorbic acid tablet, dissolve in a little water and stir into the steeping petals. Keep the container covered as much as possible! Every whiff of rose fragrance means that flavor is escaping into the air. Tie plastic over the container and allow to remain overnight to transfer the essence of roses from the petals to the must.

D. Next day, rinse your equipment with stock sterile solution (*see* How to Sterilize with Metabisulfites, page 80).

E. Line funnel or strainer with cheesecloth to catch petals as the liquid pours through into primary container. Gather up corners of the cheesecloth, squeeze the petals dry and discard.

F. Dissolve 3½ cups of sugar in 1½ cups of boiling water. Cool this syrup and add to the primary container, along with the orange juice, acid blend and yeast nutrient.

G. Take a sugar reading with your saccharometer or hydrometer (*see* Sugar Control, page 82). Specific gravity should be 1.084 or Balling 21.0. Take an acid reading with your acid titration kit (*see* Acid Control, page 85). Acid content should be

.60 percent. Adjust for sugar or acid if necessary, as explained on page 106.

H. When the must has cooled to between 72 and 78 degrees F., move the primary container to the place where the must will undergo its first fermentation. Sprinkle the yeast on top without stirring, cover with plastic and tie down tightly. Let stand overnight.

STEP TWO
DAILY CHECKS

A. This wine is unusually active, so by the time you stir in the yeast in the morning the must will no doubt be bubbling and whispering. Stir the must daily (tying the plastic down each time) and take a saccharometer or hydrometer reading each day after the second day. This wine may surprise you with its rapid fermentation, so if you are planning a long weekend away from home, it might be wiser to rack a little ahead of time or even before the sugar reading has dropped to specific gravity 1.026 (Balling: 7.0).

STEP THREE
FIRST RACKING

INGREDIENTS
2 Cups water
½ Cup sugar
½ Campden tablet

EQUIPMENT
1-gallon glass jar or jug
Siphon hose
Air lock

A. Before beginning to rack, bring 2 cups of water to a boil, add ½ cup of sugar and stir until thoroughly dissolved.

B. While syrup cools, sterilize equipment (*see* How to Sterilize with Metabisulfites, page 80).

C. Crush ½ Campden tablet in a little water and pour into gallon jug. Rack must into the jar rather quietly (*see* How to Rack Wines, First Racking, page 87). Too much splashing encourages oxidation, which may impair the exquisite color and bouquet of this wine.

D. Top off with the cooled sugar syrup (*see* Topping Off, page 91) and apply an air lock (*see* How to Fit an Air Lock, page 93).

E. Ferment for 3 weeks, or until the wine begins to clear and there is about a ½-inch deposit of sludge at the bottom of the jug.

STEP FOUR
SECOND RACKING

INGREDIENTS
½ Campden tablet

EQUIPMENT
1-gallon glass jug or jar
Siphon hose
Air lock

A. Sterilize equipment (see page 80).

B. Crush ½ Campden tablet in 1 cup of water and pour into the gallon jug. Rack as quietly as possible (see How to Rack Wines, page 89).

C. If topping off is required, do so with a sugar syrup made from 2 cups of boiling water mixed with ¼ cup sugar. Cool the syrup before adding to the wine.

D. Apply an air lock (see page 93).

E. Store wine in a cool, dark spot. Ferment for 3 months.

STEP FIVE
THIRD RACKING

INGREDIENTS
½ Campden tablet

EQUIPMENT
1-gallon glass jug or jar
Siphon hose
Air lock

A. Sterilize jug, hose and air lock with stock metabisulfite solution (see page 80).

B. Crush ½ Campden tablet in ½ cup of tap water and add it to the jug. Rack the wine into the clean jug, leaving *all* sediment behind.

C. Top off with tepid water if necessary and seal with air lock.

D. Store in a cool, dark place until perfectly clear (about 6 to 9 months).

E. Check with a Candle Test (*see* page 95) to determine if wine is ready to bottle.

STEP SIX
BOTTLING THE WINE

EQUIPMENT
5 25-ounce wine bottles or
4 25-ounce wine bottles and 2 half-bottles
Siphon hose
Appropriate closures

A. Directions for bottling are given in the How to Bottle Wines section (*see* page 99).

STEP SEVEN
STORING AND AGING THE WINE

A. General instructions for storing and aging your wine appear on page 101.

B. Store for 4 to 6 months, then sample a small bottle. If the wine still tastes a little raw, age the remaining bottles for 3 months, then sample again.

STRAWBERRY WINE

If you think strawberry wine must be cloying and syrupy sweet—think again. This is perhaps the most fascinating wine you will *ever* taste—slightly dry and very delicate, with a subtle strawberry flavor that lingers on the back of your tongue after each sip. Take advantage of late-spring harvest prices or your own surplus crop to turn fresh strawberries into nectar.

(Yield: 1 gallon)

STEP ONE
PRIMARY FERMENTATION

INGREDIENTS
4 Pints fresh strawberries
2 Quarts cold water
1⅓ Cups sugar
2 Quarts hot water
⅓ Teaspoon grape tannin
4½ Teaspoons acid blend
½ Teaspoon pectic enzyme powder
¾ Teaspoon yeast nutrient
1 Package self-starting all-purpose wine yeast

EQUIPMENT
Equipment as listed in Basic Equipment for
Primary Fermentation, *see* page 6

A. Set out and sterilize your primary fermentation equipment (*see* How to Sterilize with Metabisulfites, page 80).

B. Thoroughly rinse firm, fully ripe strawberries and drain well. Hull berries, cut in quarters and place in a large bowl. Crush with a wooden or ceramic pestle or purée in a blender. Pour the thoroughly crushed strawberries into the primary container. Mix sugar with 2 quarts of hot water and add this syrup to the primary container. Stir in grape tannin, acid blend, pectic enzyme powder and yeast nutrient.

C. Cool the must to between 72 and 78 degrees F. before adding the yeast. In the meanwhile, withdraw a must sample with your plastic baster and test it for sugar content with a hydrometer or saccharometer (see Sugar Control, page 82). Specific gravity should be 1.088 or Balling 22.0. Titrate for acid content with the acid titration kit (see Acid Control, page 85). Acid content should be .55 percent. Make adjustments for sugar or acid if needed.

D. Set the primary container where it will undergo primary fermentation, sprinkle the yeast over the must without stirring, and tie the plastic sheeting down securely. Allow the yeast to lie on the surface of the must for 12 hours, then stir in thoroughly and re-tie plastic covering. Ferment for 1 week, stirring daily.

STEP TWO
FIRST RACKING

INGREDIENTS
½ Campden tablet

EQUIPMENT
1-gallon glass jug or jar

Large plastic funnel with fine-mesh nylon strainer
Fine-mesh nylon bag or clean stocking
Wooden spoon
Small glass measuring cup with handle
Air lock

A. At this stage it is impossible to rack Strawberry Wine in the usual manner. Bits of berry and seeds would clog the siphon hose; so you must proceed a little differently here. Sterilize all equipment as usual with stock metabisulfite solution (*see* page 80).

B. Set the glass jug alongside the primary container and insert the plastic funnel in its neck. Drape a fine-mesh nylon bag or a brand new nylon stocking over the top of the funnel to catch the pulp and seeds. Use a cup to transfer the must. Try not to include any yeasty sediment. As the bag (or the toe of the stocking) fills, squeeze dry and discard used pulp. Remember, this process takes the place of racking and should be handled accordingly (*see* How to Rack Wines, First Racking, page 87).

C. As soon as the last drop has been extracted from the seeds and pulp, remove funnel and seal jug with an air lock (*see* How to Fit an Air Lock, page 93). Transfer any surplus must to a smaller glass container and add ½ crushed Campden tablet. Fit this smaller bottle with an air lock also. (This extra must is useful in topping off in subsequent rackings.) Allow the must to ferment undisturbed for 3 weeks.

STEP THREE
SECOND RACKING

INGREDIENTS
½ Campden tablet

½ 100-milligram ascorbic acid tablet
⅔ Cup water

EQUIPMENT
1-gallon glass jug or jar
Siphon hose
Air lock

A. Sterilize the equipment with stock metabisulfite solution (*see* page 80).

B. Crush ½ Campden tablet and ½ ascorbic acid tablet in ⅔ cup of water and add to the sterilized jug. Rack the wine carefully, allowing it to flow smoothly off its sediment (*see* How to Rack Wines, Second Racking, page 89). Top off with surplus wine or with tap water. Fill sterile air lock with fresh metabisulfite solution and fit to jug. Rack any wine left in the surplus bottle to a smaller sterilized bottle and seal with an air lock. Set the wine in a cool, dark storage place for 3 months to ferment and clear.

STEP FOUR
THIRD RACKING

INGREDIENTS
½ Campden tablet

EQUIPMENT
1-gallon glass jug or jar
Siphon hose
Air lock

A. Sterilize all equipment (*see* page 80).

B. Crush ½ Campden tablet in a tablespoon of tap water and add to the sterilized jug. Rack carefully, leaving all sediment behind (see How to Rack Wines, Third Racking, page 89). Top off with surplus wine or plain tap water. Fit the jug with freshly filled air lock. Store in a cool, dark spot for 4 to 6 months. After 4 months do a Candle Test (see Candle Test, page 95). If the flame appears sharp and distinct and there are no surface bubbles, the wine is ready to be bottled. If wine appears hazy, fill air lock with fresh sterile solution, leave the wine undisturbed for 2 more months, then re-test.

STEP FIVE
BOTTLING THE WINE

EQUIPMENT
5 25-ounce wine bottles or
4 25-ounce wine bottles and 2 half-bottles
Siphon hose
Appropriate closures for each bottle

A. Wines should be brilliantly clear before bottling, with no suggestion of cloudiness or particles in suspension. Most wines, given a chance, will clear of their own accord. If yours proves stubborn, fining your wine will probably clear it (see Fining, page 97).

B. Directions for bottling are given in How to Bottle Wines (see page 99).

STEP SIX
STORING AND AGING THE WINE

Age for 4 to 6 months, then sample a small bottle. If the wine is mellow and pleasing, enjoy the remaining bottles at your leisure. Should your wine taste a little raw around the edges, it will need further aging. Sample another half-bottle in 2 to 3 months. White (grape) wines, fruit wines and flower wines generally are ready for drinking well inside of a year.

DATE WINE

Sugary, unsulfured dates lend subtle flavor to this full-bodied, rather dry wine. A natural-food store is naturally the place to look for unsulfured dates, but you may sometimes find them tucked away on your grocer's shelf.

(Yield: 1 gallon)

STEP ONE
PRIMARY FERMENTATION

INGREDIENTS
2¾ Pounds fresh dates
2 Cups sugar
1 Gallon plus 1 cup water
2 Teaspoons citric acid
4 Teaspoons acid blend
1¼ Teaspoons tartaric acid
1 Teaspoon yeast nutrient
¾ Teaspoon grape tannin
¾ Teaspoon pectic enzyme powder
½ Campden tablet
1 Package self-starting all-purpose wine
yeast

EQUIPMENT
You'll need only the equipment listed in the Basic Equipment for Primary Fermentation, *see* page 6

A. Sterilize equipment with stock metabisulfite solution (*see* How to Sterilize with Metabisulfites, page 80).

B. Use a sharp stainless-steel knife to chop dates into small dice. Place chopped dates in the primary container and add sugar, water, acids, yeast nutrient, grape tannin and pectic enzymes.

C. Crush ½ Campden tablet in a little water and mix into the must. Stir until ingredients are well blended.

D. Cool the must to between 72 and 78 degrees F. before adding the yeast.

E. While the must cools, withdraw a sample (be sure to include no large pieces of date) with the plastic baster and test for sugar content with your hydrometer or saccharometer (see Sugar Control, page 82). Specific gravity should be 1.094 or Balling 23.0. Adjust for sugar as indicated. Test for total acids with your acid titration kit (see Acid Control, page 85). Acid content should be .60 percent. Adjust for acid if necessary.

F. Set primary container where it is to undergo primary fermentation, sprinkle yeast over the top, and cover tightly with a sheet of plastic. Allow the yeast to work on the surface of the must for 12 hours, then stir in thoroughly and re-tie plastic covering.

STEP TWO
DAILY CHECKS

Stir the must once daily for 7 or 8 days, checking progress with the hydrometer or saccharometer each day after the second day. When the specific gravity drops to 1.026 (Balling: 7.0), the must is ready for the first racking.

STEP THREE
FIRST RACKING

EQUIPMENT
1-gallon glass jug or jar
Large plastic funnel with fine-mesh nylon strainer
Fine-mesh nylon bag or clean nylon stocking
Wooden spoon
Small glass measuring cup with handle
Air lock

A. Sterilize all equipment (*see* page 80).

B. Since floating pulp makes it impossible to rack Date Wine in the usual manner at this stage, you must proceed a little differently. Place the clean glass jug alongside the primary container and insert the plastic funnel in its neck. Drape a fine-mesh nylon bag or a brand-new nylon stocking over the top of the funnel.

C. Use a cup to transfer the must, taking care to leave all of the yeasty sediment behind. Remember, this process takes the place of racking and should be handled accordingly (*see* page 87).

D. As the bag or toe of the stocking fills with pulp, squeeze out and discard dry pulp. Replace the bag or stocking inside the funnel and repeat the process.

E. As soon as the jug has been filled to the neck, remove the funnel and attach air lock.

F. Any surplus must should be strained, stored in a smaller jug or bottle and closed with an air lock also. This extra must will come in handy for topping off at subsequent rackings.

G. Allow the must to ferment and clear undisturbed for 4 weeks, then rack again.

STEP FOUR
SECOND RACKING

INGREDIENTS
2 Cups water
½ Cup sugar
½ Campden tablet

EQUIPMENT
1-gallon glass jug or jar
Siphon hose
Air lock

A. Sterilize equipment (*see* page 80).

B. Heat water, add sugar and stir until dissolved. Mix crushed ½ Campden tablet into the cooled syrup.

C. Rack the wine (*see* Second Racking, page 89) into the clean jug, lowering the free end of the siphon hose all the way to the bottom of the jug so that the wine flows out quietly.

D. Top off (*see* Topping Off, page 91) with cooled sugar syrup or with surplus wine left over from the first racking.

E. Seal jug with air lock and set in a cool, dark storage place for 3 months to ferment undisturbed.

STEP FIVE
THIRD RACKING

INGREDIENTS
½ Campden tablet

EQUIPMENT
1-gallon glass jug or jar
Siphon hose
Air lock

A. Sterilize equipment (*see* page 80).

B. Crush ½ Campden tablet in a little water and pour into jug.

C. Rack wine in a quiet flow so that it has little or no exposure to air. Leave all sediment behind. (*See* How to Rack Wines, Third Racking, page 89).

D. Top off (*see* Topping Off, page 91), fit jug with air lock and return to cool, dark storage place until clear (usually 4 to 6 months).

STEP SIX
CANDLE TEST

As the months go by and fermentation ceases, the wine will gradually clear. Apply a Candle Test (*see* Candle Test, page 95). If wine is not perfectly clear, put fresh solution in air lock and let stand for 2 more months, then re-do Candle Test.

STEP SEVEN
BOTTLING THE WINE

EQUIPMENT
5 25-ounce wine bottles or
4 25-ounce wine bottles and 2 half-bottles
Siphon hose
Appropriate closures

When your wine is brilliantly clear and absolutely stable, bottle it according to the instructions given in How to Bottle Wines (page 99).

STEP EIGHT
STORING AND AGING THE WINE

General instructions for storing and aging your wine appear on page 101

Date wine is rather slow to ripen and may be sampled 6 to 8 months after bottling. If the wine still has a raw edge, age a few months longer.

PEACH WINE

A delicate, slightly sweet wine, as clear and glowing as liquid gold. Who would believe it all began with two commonplace cans of peaches from a supermarket shelf?
(Yield: 1 gallon)

STEP ONE
PRIMARY FERMENTATION

INGREDIENTS
2 29-ounce cans peaches in sugar syrup
3¼ Quarts water
4½ Cups sugar
¾ Cup orange juice
6½ Teaspoons acid blend
1 Teaspoon yeast nutrient
½ Campden tablet
½ Teaspoon pectic enzyme powder
¼ Teaspoon grape tannin
1 Package self-starting all-purpose wine
yeast

EQUIPMENT
Basic Equipment List for Primary
Fermentation, see page 6

A. Rinse all equipment with your stock metabisulfite solution (see How to Sterilize with Metabisulfites, page 80).

B. Squish the peaches in your hands, use a wooden pestle or purée in an electric blender. (In this case, sterilize the blender too). You should end up with about 7½ cups of blended fruit and juice in the primary container.

C. Heat the water, dissolve the sugar in it, and allow to cool a bit. Add this syrup to the peach purée along with the orange juice, yeast nutrient, ½ Campden tablet crushed in a table-spoon of water, pectic enzyme powder and grape tannin. Stir until thoroughly mixed.

D. Withdraw a must sample with your plastic baster and test for sugar content with a hydrometer or saccharometer (*see* Sugar Control, page 82). Specific gravity should be 1.094 or Balling 23.0. Titrate for acid content with your acid titration kit (*see* Acid Control, page 85). Acid content should be .65 per-cent. Make necessary adjustments for sugar or acid.

E. Set primary container where it is to undergo primary fer-mentation. As soon as the must temperature is 72 to 78 degrees F., sprinkle the yeast over the top but do not stir in. Cover primary container tightly with plastic sheeting and allow yeast to work for 12 hours. Stir yeast in thoroughly and re-tie plastic covering.

F. Stir the must daily for 5 days, or until specific gravity drops to 1.030 or the Balling scale measures 8.0. Re-tie plastic each time.

STEP TWO
FIRST RACKING

INGREDIENTS
1 Cup sugar

3 Cups boiling water
½ Campden tablet

EQUIPMENT
1-gallon glass jug or jar
Siphon hose
Air lock

A. Dissolve sugar in 3 cups boiling water and set aside to cool.

B. Sterilize equipment with metabisulfites (*see* How to Sterilize with Metabisulfites, page 80).

C. Crush ½ Campden tablet in 1 tablespoon of water and pour into sterilized jug. Rack the must off its sediment into jug, allowing it to splash as it flows out of the hose (*see* How to Rack Wines, First Racking, page 87). Top off with sugar syrup (*see* page 91) and attach the clean air lock (*see* How to Fit an Air Lock, page 93). Set the wine in a cool, dark storage place to ferment undisturbed for 3 weeks, then rack again.

STEP THREE
SECOND RACKING

INGREDIENTS
½ Campden tablet

EQUIPMENT
1-gallon glass jug or jar
Siphon hose
Air lock

A. Sterilize equipment with stock metabisulfite solution (*see* page 80).

B. Crush ½ Campden tablet in 1 tablespoon of water and add to jug. Rack wine carefully (*see* How to Rack Wines, Second Racking, page 89).

C. Top off with tap water and seal with freshly filled air lock. Place wine in cool, dark storage place for 3 months to clear.

STEP FOUR
THIRD RACKING

INGREDIENTS
½ Campden tablet

EQUIPMENT
1-gallon glass jug or jar
Siphon hose
Air lock

A. Sterilize equipment with stock metabisulfite solution (*see* page 80).

B. Crush ½ Campden tablet in tablespoon of tap water and add it to jug. Rack wine very quietly, taking care to leave all sediment behind (*see* How to Rack Wines, Third Racking, page 89).

C. Top off with tap water and fit with freshly filled air lock before returning wine to its cool, dark storage place.

STEP FIVE
CANDLE TEST

It should take 3 to 5 months for this wine to finish its fermentation and clear sufficiently for bottling. Check for clarity after 3 months by doing a Candle Test (*see* Candle Test, page 95). If the flame seems hazy or there are surface bubbles, empty air lock, fill with fresh sterile solution, and leave the wine undisturbed 2 months more.

STEP SIX
BOTTLING THE WINE

EQUIPMENT
5 25-ounce wine bottles or
4 25-ounce bottles and 2 half-bottles
Siphon hose
Appropriate closures for each bottle

A. Wines should be brilliant and clear before bottling, with no suggestion of cloudiness or particles in suspension. Directions for bottling are supplied in the How to Bottle Wines section (*see* page 99).

B. Age for 4 to 6 months before sampling a small bottle to decide whether it needs further aging. I generally age this wine only 3 to 5 months in the bottle.

FULL-BODIED APPLE WINE USING FROZEN APPLE JUICE CONCENTRATE

Concentrated frozen apple juice from your supermarket is incredibly easy to use. It produces an excellent, pure-gold wine with the full-bodied tang and tantalizing aroma of fresh apples. (Yield: 1 gallon)

STEP ONE
PRIMARY FERMENTATION

INGREDIENTS
2 6-ounce cans frozen apple juice concentrate
10½ Cups very cold water
4 Cups hot water
4⅓ Cups granulated sugar
6 Teaspoons acid blend
1 Campden tablet
1 Teaspoon yeast nutrient
½ Teaspoon pectic enzyme
¼ Teaspoon grape tannin (mix to a paste with 2 tablespoons water)
1 Package self-starting all-purpose wine yeast

EQUIPMENT
Can opener
Equipment as listed in Basic Equipment for Primary Fermentation, *see* page 6

A. Use your stock metabisulfite solution (*see* How to Sterilize with Metabisulfites, page 80) to sterilize all equipment, including tops of concentrate cans and can opener.

B. Empty apple juice concentrate and cold water into primary container. Measure the hot water into a glass pot and dissolve sugar over a low flame.

C. Add hot sugar syrup to the apple juice and stir. Add all remaining ingredients *except yeast.* Stir until well mixed. Cool to 72 to 78 degrees F.

D. While the must is cooling, withdraw a sample and use your hydrometer or saccharometer to test for sugar (*see* Sugar Control, page 82). Specific gravity should be 1.094 or Balling 23.0. Withdraw another sample and titrate for acid content (*see* Acid Control, page 85). Acid content should be .65 percent. Adjust for sugar or acid if necessary.

STEP TWO
CONTINUING...

Before adding the yeast, set the primary container where it will remain during fermentation. (Any joggling about after the yeast has been added will cause the yeast to stick to the container's sides.) Sprinkle the yeast onto must, tie plastic sheeting securely over container top, and allow to work for 12 hours. Remove plastic sheet, stir well, then re-cover and tie down tightly again.

STEP THREE
DAILY CHECKS

Stir daily for 4 to 5 days, taking a sugar reading every day after the second day. When the specific gravity drops to 1.030 (Balling: 8.0), the must is ready for first racking.

STEP FOUR
FIRST RACKING

INGREDIENTS
¾ Cup sugar
2 Cups boiling water

EQUIPMENT
1-gallon glass jug or jar
Siphon hose
Air lock

A. Sterilize equipment with stock metabisulfite solution (*see* page 80).

B. Rack the must into the gallon jug, taking care not to include any of the sediment (*see* How to Rack Wines, page 87).

C. Should your must need topping off (*see* Topping Off, page 91) prepare a syrup by dissolving ¾ cup sugar in 2 cups boiling water. Cool before adding to jug.

D. Seal jug with air lock and allow must to ferment for 3 to 4 weeks, or until it is fairly clear.

STEP FIVE
SECOND RACKING

INGREDIENTS
½ Campden tablet

EQUIPMENT
1-gallon glass jug or jar
Siphon hose
Air lock

A. Sterilize jug, hose and air lock with stock metabisulfite solution (*see* page 80).

B. Crush ½ Campden tablet with a little water and pour solution into jug.

C. Rack wine off its sediment and into clean jug, lowering the free end of the siphon hose to the bottom so that the wine flows quietly. Top off with tap water if necessary (*see* page 92).

D. Seal with the air lock and set jug in a cool, dark place for 3 months.

STEP SIX
THIRD RACKING

INGREDIENTS
½ Campden tablet

EQUIPMENT
1-gallon glass jug or jar
Siphon hose
Air lock

A. Sterilize equipment needed for racking (*see* page 80).

B. Crush ½ Campden tablet in ½ cup of water and pour mixture into clean jug. Rack wine, allowing it to flow quietly (*see* page 89). Bend the tube to slow down the flow if the wine bubbles in the jar.

C. Top off with tepid tap water. Fill the air lock with fresh sulfite solution and fit securely to top of jug (*see* page 93).

D. The wine now needs time to conclude its fermentation and to clear. Place in a cool, dark storage spot for about 6 months. At the end of that time test for clarity (*see* Candle Test, page 95). If wine is not perfectly clear, change solution in air lock and allow to age for 2 months more, or until it passes the Candle Test.

STEP SEVEN
BOTTLING THE WINE

EQUIPMENT
5 25-ounce wine bottles or
4 25-ounce bottles and 2 half-bottles
Siphon hose
Appropriate closures for each bottle

A. When you are sure all fermentation has ceased and wine is brilliantly clear, proceed according to the directions indicated in the section on How to Bottle Wines (*see* page 99).

STEP EIGHT
STORING AND AGING YOUR WINE

Full-Bodied Apple Wine rarely fails to mature quickly. It is usually ready to drink after 3 to 4 months in the bottle.

WHITE WINE FROM FRESH WHITE GRAPES

If you grow your own grapes, have access to a vineyard or happen upon some of the sale-priced fresh fruit in your super-market, you really should give this great white wine a try. This recipe produces a full-bodied, slightly dry wine with a fascinating pale-green tinge.

(Yield: 1 half-gallon)

STEP ONE
PRIMARY FERMENTATION

INGREDIENTS
8 Pounds white seedless grapes
1 Campden tablet
2½ Cups sugar
1½ Quarts hot water
1 Teaspoon yeast nutrient
½ Package self-starting all-purpose wine
yeast

EQUIPMENT
Large plastic or glass bowl
Cheesecloth or brand-new nylon
stocking
Large nylon strainer or funnel with fine-
mesh nylon strainer
Plus equipment listed in Basic Equipment
for Primary Fermentation (see page 6)

A. Although purists insist that the wild yeasts naturally present on grape skins are a great asset to fermentation, please do wash your fruit thoroughly. I haven't seen a grape in years that didn't bear some telltale signs of herbicide spraying. Your wine yeast will compensate admirably for any wild yeast that may be washed away.

B. Sterilize all equipment (*see* How to Sterilize with Metabisulfites, page 80).

C. Discard stems and place grapes in a large bowl. Mash and squeeze these a few at a time between your fingers, allowing the juice to fall into bowl. Strain juice into primary container through a funnel lined with cheesecloth or a clean nylon stocking. Squeeze cheesecloth (or stocking) with the crushed grapes until pulp is dry. Discard pulp. White wines are *never* fermented on the pulp. Crush Campden tablet in a little water and stir it in thoroughly.

D. Dissolve sugar in 1½ quarts of hot water, allow to cool, and add to primary container along with yeast nutrient. Mix ingredients well.

E. Withdraw a sample of the must with your gravy baster and test it for sugar content with a hydrometer or saccharometer (*see* Sugar Control, page 82). Specific gravity should be 1.090 or Balling 22.5. Withdraw another sample with the syringe from your acid titration kit and test for acid content (*see* Acid Control, page 85). Acid content should be .70 percent. Make adjustments for sugar and acid if necessary.

F. Cover primary container tightly with plastic sheeting secured with string or large rubber band, and allow must to stand for 24 hours.

STEP TWO
CONTINUING...

A. The next day sprinkle the yeast over surface of must and re-cover primary container tightly. Expose must to as little air as possible—oxidation is harmful to this wine. Allow yeast to work on the must surface for 12 hours, then stir in thoroughly and tightly re-cover.

B. Stir daily for 4 to 5 days, taking a sugar reading every day after the second day. When the specific gravity drops to 1.020 (Balling: 5.0), the must is ready for its first racking.

STEP THREE
FIRST RACKING

INGREDIENTS
¼ Campden tablet

EQUIPMENT
½-gallon glass jug or jar
Siphon hose
Air lock

A. Sterilize equipment with stock metabisulfite solution (*see* page 80).

B. Crush ¼ Campden tablet in 1 tablespoon of water and pour into sterile jug. Rack wine (*see* How to Rack Wines, First Racking, page 87). Take care not to siphon up any of the yeasty sediment.

C. Top off with tepid tap water if necessary (*see* Topping Off, page 91). Attach air lock filled with stock metabisulfite solution and set jug aside in a cool, dark spot to ferment undisturbed for 3 weeks.

STEP FOUR
SECOND RACKING

INGREDIENTS
3 Tablespoons sugar
1 Cup water
¼ Campden tablet

EQUIPMENT
½-gallon glass jug or jar
Siphon hose
Air lock

A. Dissolve sugar in 1 cup boiling water. Set syrup aside to cool.

B. Sterilize equipment with stock metabisulfite solution (page 80).

C. Crush the ¼ Campden tablet in 1 tablespoon of water and add to sterile jug. Rack wine quietly off its sediment (*see* How to Rack Wines, page 87).

D. Top off with cooled syrup and seal with freshly-filled air lock. Set wine in cool, dark storage place and continue to ferment for 3 months.

STEP FIVE
THIRD RACKING

INGREDIENTS
¼ Campden tablet

EQUIPMENT
½-gallon glass jug or jar
Siphon hose
Air lock

A. Sterilize equipment with stock metabisulfite solution (*see* page 80).

B. Crush ¼ Campden tablet in 1 tablespoon of water and add to sterile jug. Gently rack wine off its sediment (*see* How to Rack Wines, page 89) and top off with tepid tap water (*see* Topping Off, page 92). Fit jug with a freshly-filled air lock before returning to storage place to ferment for 5 months.

STEP SIX
CANDLE TEST

The wine will gradually clear as the months go by and fermentation comes to an end. Check its progress after 5 months by doing a Candle Test, page 95. Should any cloudiness or bubbles be revealed, replace the stale metabisulfite solution in the air lock with fresh solution and allow the wine 2 more months to clear. Make subsequent candle tests until wine is perfectly clear and stable.

STEP SEVEN
BOTTLING AND STORING YOUR WINES

EQUIPMENT
2 25-ounce wine bottles
1 Half-bottle
Siphon hose
Corks to fit

A. Grape wines should *generally* be chilled to precipitate the tartrate crystals that quite frequently form, so chill your wine for a few days after you are sure it is clear and stable before bottling.

B. Sterilize *all* equipment (*see* page 80).

C. Rack the wine off the tartrate crystals and into bottles as directed in the How to Bottle Wines section (*see* page 99). Allow the wine to flow quietly into the bottles. Fit with suitable corks. Store bottles on their sides in a cool, dark storage bin.

White grape wines usually require up to one year's aging in the bottle to develop full bouquet and flavor, but a few mature after only 6 to 8 months. Sample the half-bottle in 6 months and make a calculated guess as to when the others will be ready. Take into consideration that small bottles age a bit faster than larger ones.

DRY RED WINE FROM FRESH RED GRAPES

If you live near an inexpensive source of supply, you might want to try the following recipe for rosé and red wines. Though making a really fine red wine tends to be a bit more "iffy" than making other types, a combination of superior grapes, correct sugar and acid levels and a fair amount of luck will produce a fantastic wine. And no matter what, you'll end up with a tolerable wine and the enjoyment and experience of making it.

The best choice of grapes is equal quantities of high-sugar, low-acid vinifera grapes and low-sugar, high-acid hybrid varieties; however, try your luck with any available grapes. It is absolutely necessary to test and correct the sugar and acid content of the must.

(Yield: 1 gallon first-run wine and 1 gallon second-run or false wine, page 69)

STEP ONE
PRIMARY FERMENTATION

INGREDIENTS

7 Pounds vinifera grapes (or other)
7 Pounds hybrid grapes (or other)
Acid blend as needed to adjust the acid content
Sugar and water as needed to adjust the sugar content
1 Campden tablet
1 Teaspoon yeast nutrient

½ Teaspoon pectic enzyme powder
1 Package self-starting all-purpose wine
yeast

EQUIPMENT

Equipment as listed in Basic Equipment for
Primary Fermentation, *see* page 6.

A. Use your stock metabisulfite solution (*see* How to Sterilize with Metabisulfites, page 80) to sterilize all equipment.

B. Stem the grapes. Working with a few at a time over the primary container, press the grapes with your fingers until the skins snap, then drop the fruit into the container. When all grapes have been processed, squeeze and pound the fruit to extract as much juice as possible. If you're making several gallons, use a wooden masher. Add all remaining ingredients, except the yeast, to the must.

C. Withdraw a must sample and use your hydrometer or saccharometer to test for sugar (*see* Sugar Control, page 82). Specific gravity should be 1.088 (Balling: 22.0). Withdraw another sample and titrate for acid content (*see* Acid Control, page 85). Acid content should be .65 percent. Adjust for sugar or acid if necessary.

STEP TWO
CONTINUING . . .

Before adding yeast, set primary container where it will undergo fermentation. (Any joggling after the yeast has been added causes the yeast to stick to the container sides.) Sprinkle yeast over must surface and tie plastic sheeting securely over container top. Do not stir yeast in. Allow the yeast to work undisturbed for 12 hours. Remove plastic sheet, stir well, then re-cover and tie top down tightly. Ferment to the color and body you prefer, according to the following chart:

> For a rosé wine, ferment for 12 hours.
> For a light-red wine, ferment for 2 days.
> For a medium-red wine, ferment for 3 days.
> For a dark robust red wine, ferment for 5 to 6 days.

If you're making a darker wine, stir the must daily. Re-cover each time. Do not stir the must for 12 hours prior to racking.

STEP THREE
FIRST RACKING

EQUIPMENT

1-gallon glass jug
Large plastic funnel
Fine-mesh nylon bag, new nylon stocking or
cheesecloth
Small glass measuring cup with handle
Air lock

A. Sterilize all equipment as usual with stock metabisulfite solution (see page 80).

B. At this stage it is impossible to rack the wine in the usual manner, since skins and seeds may clog the siphon hose. Instead, proceed as follows. Set the glass jug alongside the primary container and place the funnel in its neck. Line the funnel with nylon bag, stocking or cheesecloth to catch the skin and seeds. Use a cup to transfer the must a bit at a time. Leave behind as much yeast sediment as possible. As the funnel liner fills, squeeze to extract the juice. Reserve the skins for making second or false wine.

C. Fill the jug only ⅞ full, since the yeast content will be high and fermentation may be quite active. Attach an air lock (*see* How to Fit an Air Lock, page 93) and continue fermenting for 10 days; then rack again.

STEP FOUR
SECOND RACKING

EQUIPMENT
1-gallon glass jug
Siphon hose
Air lock

A. Sterilize the equipment with stock metabisulfite solution (*see* page 80).

B. Gently rack wine off its heavy deposit of sediment (*see* How to Rack Wines, page 89). Do not top off at this point. Fit with a freshly filled air lock and set aside in a cool, dark place for 3 weeks. Top off with tepid tap water and refit air lock. Rack again in 2 months.

STEP FIVE
THIRD RACKING

INGREDIENTS
½ Campden tablet

EQUIPMENT
1-gallon glass jug
Siphon hose
Air lock

A. Sterilize equipment with stock metabisulfite solution (*see* page 80).

B. Crush ½ Campden tablet in 1 tablespoon of water and add to sterile jug. Quietly rack wine off sediment (*see* How to Rack Wines, page 89). Top off with tepid tap water (*see* Topping Off, page 92), or with a sugar syrup (*see* page 91) if a sweeter wine is desired. Fit jug with a freshly filled air lock before returning to storage place to continue fermentation for 6 months.

STEP SIX
CANDLE TEST

The wine will gradually clear as the months go by and fermentation comes to an end. Check after 6 months by doing a Candle Test, page 95. Should any cloudiness or bubbles be revealed, replace the stale metabisulfite solution in the air lock with fresh solution and allow the wine 2 more months to clear. Make subsequent candle tests until wine is perfectly clear and stable.

STEP SEVEN
BOTTLING AND STORING YOUR WINES

EQUIPMENT
5 25-ounce wine bottles or

4 25-ounce wine bottles and 2 half-bottles
Siphon hose
Corks to fit

A. Sterilize all equipment (*see* page 80).

B. Grape wine should generally be chilled at about 40 degrees F. for several days prior to bottling to precipitate tartrate crystals that are apt to form.

C. Rack the wine into bottles as directed in the How to Bottle Wines section (*see* page 99). Fit with corks. Store bottles on their sides in a cool, dark storage bin.
Red grape wines usually develop superior bouquet and flavor if allowed to age in the bottle for at least 1 year. Sample a bottle at the expiration of that time. Age further if the wine tastes raw.

SECOND OR FALSE WINE

By using the skins and the partly fermented wine left behind in your container after the first racking and adding a little sugar, you can double the volume of your wine. Second wine is a bit lighter in body than first-run wine but it can be every bit as good. An added bonus is that it is usually ready to drink much sooner than its parent wine. If your taste runs to really light-bodied wines you can even try for a third-run wine from the original grapeskins.

(Yield: 1 gallon second wine)

STEP ONE
PRIMARY FERMENTATION

INGREDIENTS
Water
4 Cups sugar
3 Teaspoons acid blend
1 Teaspoon yeast nutrient
¼ Teaspoon grape tannin

EQUIPMENT
Equipment as listed in Basic Equipment for
Primary Fermentation (see page 6).

A. After racking the original red wine (see Dry Red Wine from Fresh Grapes, Step Three, page 65), return the skins to the primary container. There should be some juice and yeasty sediment left behind in the container. Add water in equal amount to the wine you racked into the jug (secondary container). Stir in the sugar, acid blend, yeast nutrient and grape tannin.

B. Cover the container tightly with plastic and set aside to ferment. Stir the must twice a day. Make daily checks with your hydrometer or saccharometer. As soon as the specific gravity drops to 1.015 (Balling 4.0), proceed as in Dry Red Wine from Fresh Red Grapes, Steps Three through Seven, pages 65 through 68.

COMMERCIAL GRAPE CONCENTRATES

Grape concentrates have contributed enormously to the popularity of home winemaking. Commercially produced in this country and abroad, they provide the amateur with an easy, economical and almost foolproof method of making good-quality wines. Only one concentrate recipe is outlined in this book (Red Wine from Barbera Wine Concentrate, page 73) because I prefer the less expensive, more delicate and distinctive homemade wines. If you prefer more robust commercial-type wines, you will probably enjoy the taste of wines made from concentrates.

Concentrates consist of pure juices from grapes picked at the peak of perfection, vacuum-packed with most of the water removed. They contain no added sugar or preservatives. The winemaker merely restores the water that has been removed and proceeds exactly as if the juice were freshly pressed.

Concentrates may seem expensive, but when you consider the price of buying and shipping fresh fruit, plus the costly crushing and pressing equipment needed to convert large quantities of fruit into juice, you will find concentrates a surprisingly good buy.

They are also convenient to use, they store well, have practically no pulp, and leave little sediment. All concentrates are pasteurized to eliminate spoilage organisms, and many come already sterilized with SO_2 (see How to Sterilize with Metabisulfites, page 80). This added convenience makes it important for the winemaker to check the label on the concentrate package to see if SO_2 has been added at the winery. If the concentrate contains SO_2, do not add metabisulfites to the must, or the chemical concentration will inhibit the fermentation. If SO_2 has not been added, you may safely add metabisulfites, but allow the must to stand for 24 hours before adding the yeast.

RED WINE FROM BARBERA WINE CONCENTRATE

Concentrates such as this one made from California-grown red Barbera grapes have become increasingly popular with amateur winemakers because of their availability and economy. Concentrate preparation is unusually easy, practically foolproof, and produces a rich wine of professional quality. Once the water is restored to the wine, the winemaker proceeds exactly as with freshly pressed juice.

(Yield: 5 gallons)

STEP ONE
PRIMARY FERMENTATION

INGREDIENTS
1 Gallon commercial Barbera Wine
Concentrate*
2 Gallons hot (not boiling) water
2 Gallons cold water
5½ Cups sugar
6 Teaspoons yeast nutrient
1½ Teaspoons grape tannin
2 Packages self-starting all-purpose wine
yeast

EQUIPMENT
Equipment as listed in Basic Equipment for
Primary Fermentation, *see* page 6.

*Available at winemaking supply stores.

A. Before preparing the must, check the label on the concentrate container. Add metabisulfites (Campden tablets) to the must *only* if sulfur dioxide (SO_2) has *not* been added previously. In this case crush 3½ Campden tablets, mix them with ¼ cup of water, and stir the mixture into the must. Allow this must to stand tightly covered with a plastic sheet for 24 hours before adding the yeast.

B. Sterilize all equipment with stock solution (*see* How to Sterilize with Metabisulfites, page 80).

C. Open the concentrate and pour into the primary container. Use the empty concentrate container to measure out 2 gallons of hot water. Shake container to loosen any concentrate sediment stuck in the bottom. If sediment refuses to budge, cut plastic container in half, scoop out the sediment and then stir in the 2 gallons of cold water along with sugar, yeast nutrient and grape tannin.

D. (Commercial concentrates are generally well balanced before they are bottled, so this step may be eliminated if you like. A really avid winemaker, however, would never take the chance of a slip-up.)
When ingredients are well mixed, withdraw a sample of the must and measure for sugar content (*see* Sugar Control, page 82). Specific gravity should be 1.094 or Balling 23.0. Acid content (*see* Acid Control, page 85) should be .65 percent. Make adjustments for sugar or acid if necessary.

E. When temperature of must drops to between 72 and 78

degrees F., sprinkle yeast over the surface without stirring, cover container with a sheet of plastic tightly tied down, and allow to stand for 12 hours.

STEP TWO
CONTINUING...

A. Uncover the container and stir the yeast thoroughly into the must. Re-cover the container and allow to ferment for 4 to 5 days.

STEP THREE
DAILY CHECKS

A. Check the must each day after the second day, dipping your baster through the red-purple foam to withdraw samples. As soon as the specific gravity drops to 1.030 (Balling: 8.0), the must is ready for its first racking.

STEP FOUR
FIRST RACKING

EQUIPMENT
5-gallon glass jar or carboy
Siphon hose
Air lock

A. Sterilize equipment with stock metabisulfite solution (*see* page 80).

B. The first racking (*see* How to Rack Wines, page 87) should aerate the must, so allow liquid to splash into the jar.

C. Fit the jug or jar with a suitable air lock. Should you find yourself with surplus must, rack into a smaller glass jug that can also be fitted with an air lock. Use this for topping off in subsequent rackings. Allow the wine to ferment for 3 to 4 weeks, or until the specific gravity drops to 1.000 (Balling: 0), when it will be ready for the second racking.

STEP FIVE
SECOND RACKING

INGREDIENTS
1 Campden tablet

EQUIPMENT
5-gallon glass jar or carboy
Siphon hose
Air lock

A. Sterilize all equipment (*see* page 80).

B. Crush Campden tablet in a tablespoon of water and pour mixture into jug. Rack the wine off its accumulated sediment very quietly, letting free end of the hose rest against the bottom of the clean jug.

C. Fit an air lock after topping off with surplus wine or tap water. Rack any leftover wine into an even smaller glass container and fit with an air lock.

D. Store wine in a cool, dark place for 3 months.

STEP SIX
THIRD RACKING

INGREDIENTS
1 Campden tablet

EQUIPMENT
5-gallon glass jug or carboy
Siphon hose
Air lock

A. Sterilize all equipment with stock metabisulfite solution (*see* page 80).

B. Crush Campden tablet into tablespoon of water and pour into clean jar. Rack wine in a quiet flow, leaving all sediment behind.

C. Top off with either surplus wine or plain tap water. Fit jug with clean, freshly filled air lock and leave to ferment undisturbed for 6 months.

STEP SEVEN
BOTTLING AND STORING THE WINE

EQUIPMENT
25 25-ounce wine bottles or

24 25-ounce wine bottles and 2 half-bottles
Siphon hose
Corks to fit

A. To insure that all fermentation has ceased and that the wine has achieved the required clarity, perform a Candle Test, page 95. If your wine is hazy or cloudy, or if any bubbles are present, empty air lock and re-fill with fresh metabisulfite solution. Store undisturbed for 2 or more months, then re-test.

B. Directions for bottling are supplied in the How to Bottle Your Wines section (see page 99). Rack the wine into the bottles with a quiet flow and fit with suitably sized corks.

C. Age the wine for at least 1 year, then sample a bottle to determine if it is ready to drink. If you sample a half-bottle, take into consideration that wine ages faster in small bottles than in larger ones. Age further if necessary.

THE PROCESS
DESCRIBED

HOW TO STERILIZE WITH METABISULFITES

The first step in any winemaking process is to clean and sterilize the equipment you use.

The versatile chemical sulfur dioxide (SO_2) works in two ways: one, as a sterilizing agent to maintain the scrupulous cleanliness essential to winemaking and to inhibit the growth of wild yeasts and spoilage organisms; two, as an antioxidant to prevent browning and to increase the storage life of all wines.

Sold for winemaking either as sodium metabisulfite or potassium metabisulfite (food grade), it is available as crystals or as Campden tablets. (Campden tablets are basically the same chemical as the crystals, but cost more. If you have both crystals and tablets, keep the tablets for sterilizing your musts.)

STEP ONE
MAKING A STOCK STERILIZING SOLUTION

Measure 2 ounces of metabisulfite crystals in a glass (not plastic) gallon bottle and fill with warm water. Shake well to mix. Keep the bottle tightly capped with a plastic screw top when not in use. This is your sterile solution which, if reused and carefully stored, should last many months.

STEP TWO
CLEANING YOUR EQUIPMENT

Scrub all equipment with a strong mixture of sal (washing) soda and hot water. Rinse several times under hot running water. (Never use soap, which may leave a film and give your wines an unpleasant taste.)

STEP THREE
STERILIZING YOUR EQUIPMENT

A. Shake 2 or 3 cups of sterile stock solution in your containers, jugs, etc., to sterilize them, then pour the solution back into the storage jar and cover tightly.

B. When sterilizing bottles, pour the sterile solution from one to another before returning it to the storage jar. Splash a bit of solution over the necks of jugs and bottles before you rack. Always drain equipment well.

C. To sterilize smaller pieces of equipment, pour some sterile solution into a clean primary container or large bowl and douse your funnels, spoons, hydrometer, siphon, etc. Immerse corks in sterile solution and weight them down with a heavy glass plate for at least 10 minutes. Wipe dry with a cloth dipped in sterile solution.

D. Use stock solution to fill each air lock to the half-way mark (or as directed by the manufacturer).

SUGAR CONTROL

If possible, work with a hydrometer or saccharometer when preparing your musts. Either of these instruments (which incidentally indicate the same thing) helps you to maintain the control over sugar content that insures a perfect finished wine. Should you choose not to invest in a hydrometer (or saccharometer) or find you are unable to obtain one, you can estimate sugar and acid content by adding enough sugar and lemon juice to your must to duplicate the sweet tartness of well-flavored lemonade.

HYDROMETER: The scale inside a hydrometer has markings which measure the *specific gravity* (S.G.) or heaviness of a must in comparison to the specific gravity or heaviness (density) of water. Figure the density of water at 1.000. The must will register a higher density (heavier) because of the presence of fruit solids and sugar. Alongside the specific gravity scale is another scale that shows the potential alcohol content you may expect in a finished wine.

SACCHAROMETER: Sealed within the saccharometer is a Balling or Brix scale which reads from 0 to 30, with a scale indicating potential alcohol content alongside. Generally speaking, the alcoholic content of your finished wine will be half the number indicated on the scale. A saccharometer reading of 22.0 will give you a finished wine with 11 percent alcohol.

USING THE HYDROMETER OR SACCHAROMETER

This process sounds more difficult than it really is. However, after you've done it once, you should feel comfortable with the procedure.

STEP ONE
ASSEMBLE AND STERILIZE EQUIPMENT

Hydrometer or Saccharometer
Hydrometer Jar
Plastic Gravy Baster
Wine Thermometer

STEP TWO
TAKE A SAMPLE OF THE MUST

Draw off a small sample of the must with the baster and deposit it in the hydrometer jar. Strain the sample into the jar through cheesecloth if any bits of fruit are present.

STEP THREE
TAKE THE TEMPERATURE OF THE MUST

Hydrometers and saccharometers are usually designed to be read at 59 degrees F. If the temperature of the must sample is considerably above or below this, the reading will not be accurate.

Take the temperature of the must sample with your wine thermometer. If too warm, submerge the hydrometer jar in ice water to cool the sample. If too cool, dip in warm water. Ignore a difference of a few degrees either way.

STEP FOUR
HOW TO USE THE HYDROMETER OR SACCHAROMETER

A. Set the filled hydrometer jar on a level surface and insert either the hydrometer or saccharometer. Give it a good spin to dislodge any air bubbles.

B. As soon as it is still, note the number at the lowest point where the must crosses the middle of the printed scale.

STEP FIVE
CORRECT THE SUGAR CONTENT OF THE MUST

A. If your hydrometer or saccharometer shows the same specific gravity or Balling degrees listed on your recipe, return the must sample to the primary container and proceed as directed.

B. If the specific gravity or Balling reading is above or below the number shown on your recipe, return the must sample to the primary container and adjust for sugar content. Use the chart on page 106 to determine how much sugar you will need to add to raise the sugar content. To lower the sugar content, add 1½ cups of water for each gallon of must, testing after each addition. Follow up each addition of sugar or water with another sugar test until you have reached the correct sugar content called for in your recipe. Then proceed as directed.

ACID CONTROL

To produce a perfect wine, you should determine if your musts have the proper acidity and make corrections when necessary. If you accurately follow the recipes in this book, your must will probably have a balanced acid-level. This is not certain, however, since the acid content of identical fruits may vary even within the confines of the same orchard or vineyard.

The right proportion of acids in the must guarantees a healthy ferment, a strong resistance to spoilage organisms, and a characteristically tart finished wine with good keeping qualities after bottling.

Taking an acid test is extremely easy when you use the handy, inexpensive set of instruments and chemicals called an Acid Titration Kit. If you choose not to buy this kit, or find you are unable to obtain one, you can adjust for acid content by adding enough Acid Blend (*see* page 3) or fresh lemon juice so that the must has the sweet-tart taste of well-flavored lemonade.

ACID TITRATION TEST FOR MEASURING ACID CONTENT OF WINES

With your Acid Titration Kit in front of you, you'll have fun performing this easy test. (It's something like those super-simple experiments in junior high school Chemistry I.)

Your Acid Titration Kit consists of:

    A Graduated Syringe
    A Testing Vial
    A Bottle of Sodium Hydroxide or Neutralizing Solution
    A Bottle of Phenolphthalein or Color Solution
    An Eye Dropper to measure the Color Solution
    Accurate Instructions

Follow instructions that come with your kit.

EVALUATING THE TEST AND CORRECTING THE ACID LEVEL

A. If your test indicates an acid content below the percentage indicated in the recipe (that is, the color changes completely to gray or pink after only 3 or 4 cc's of sodium hydroxide are added), acid adjustment is necessary.

B. Be sure to sterilize your syringe each time you draw a sample and dispose of each sample each time you titrate.

C. Stir a small amount of acid blend (or a 2-2-1 ratio of tartaric, citric, and malic acids) into the must, mix vigorously, and titrate again. Usually one-third of an ounce of acid blend (2½ teaspoons) will raise the acid level of 1 gallon by .3 percent.

D. Don't worry if the final acid content of your must registers *slightly* higher or lower than the percentage indicated in your recipe. Just keep in mind that it's easier to put acids in than to take them out.

E. Excess acid can be reduced by diluting your must with water, but you may need to readjust the sugar content afterwards.

F. Keep your bottles of sodium hydroxide and phenolphthalein tightly stoppered, since these chemicals deteriorate when exposed to air. Refill bottles are available at winemaking supply houses.

HOW TO RACK WINES

Racking is the simple process of transferring your must or wine from one container to another by means of a siphon hose. This process is vital in winemaking because it clears and stabilizes wine.

In racking, the must or wine is siphoned off the yeast sediment (or lees) which has accumulated on the bottom of the container or jug. If the must or wine were allowed to remain on this deposit, the dregs and expiring yeast might feed on itself and begin fermentation again. This would produce an unstable and unpleasant tasting wine.

FIRST RACKING

When racking must from the primary container to a glass jug, handle the process a bit differently than in subsequent rackings.

STEP ONE

A. Sterilize all equipment needed for racking (*see* How to Sterilize with Metabisulfites, page 80).

B. Place the primary container on a counter or tabletop. Set your clean, sterilized jug on a chair or bench 1 or 2 feet lower than the container.

STEP TWO

Slip one end of the siphon hose down into the must about 2 inches above the level of the yeast sediment. Do not stir up or disturb the sediment in any way.

STEP THREE

Place the free end of the siphon in your mouth and draw

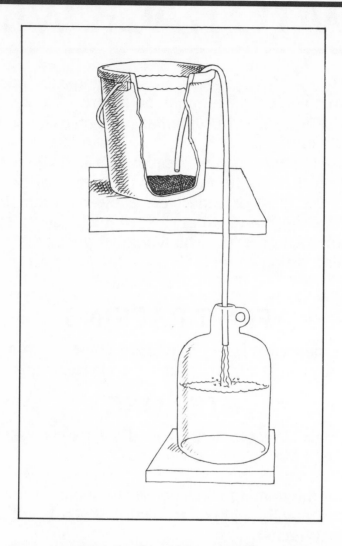

strongly once or twice so that the must flows into the siphon hose. If you do not draw on the hose strongly enough, the must will back up and disturb the yeast sediment.

STEP FOUR

As soon as the hose fills, pinch the sides together slightly at the top to slow the flow long enough for you to lower the free end of the siphon into the clean jar.

STEP FIVE

Hold the siphon about 6 inches from the bottom of the jug so that the must splashes into the jar. During the first racking the must benefits from this aeration, which releases any trapped carbon dioxide gas.

STEP SIX

When the level of the must reaches about half an inch above the sediment in the primary container (this should take no more than a minute), quickly withdraw the siphon to prevent any of the heavy sediment from being drawn into the hose. If the liquid does not fill the jug to the neck, top off (see Topping Off, page 91) and then fit with an air lock (see How to Fit an Air Lock, page 93).

SECOND AND THIRD RACKINGS

STEP ONE

Set the jug containing the wine on a counter or tabletop. Place a sterilized empty jug on a chair or bench 1 or 2 feet lower than the bottom of the wine that is to be racked.

STEP TWO

Proceed exactly as outlined in First Racking, Steps Two and Three.

STEP THREE

Lower the free end of the siphon down into the clean jug until it rests on the bottom. Release the wine in the hose by loosening your fingers. The wine will flow out quietly to fill the jug. It is important during these subsequent rackings to expose the wine to as little air as possible.

STEP FOUR

Proceed as outlined in First Racking, Step Six.

TOPPING OFF

Whenever you rack a must or wine, the jug or carboy into which it flows must be filled to the bottom of the neck so that the top surface of the wine is not overexposed to air. Since racking the wine off its sediment always results in a drop in volume, here are various methods to add to, or top off, the wine in its secondary container.

METHOD ONE
USING SURPLUS MUST OR WINE

A. After the first racking a quantity of juice sometimes remains. Rack this surplus off the sediment and into a smaller sterile jug or jar. Fill to the neck and attach an air lock. Store with the larger jar.

B. Each subsequent time you rack the wine, top off with as much of this surplus as necessary. As this surplus diminishes, transfer it to a smaller bottle or jar and fit with an air lock.

METHOD TWO
USING SUGAR SYRUP

A. If you should find yourself without surplus wine at the first and second rackings, you can make up a sugar syrup using the same proportion of sugar to water as in the original recipe.

Let's say the must contained 2 pounds of sugar to 1 gallon of liquid. To make 2 cups of sugar syrup, dissolve 4 ounces (½ cup) of sugar in 2 cups of boiling water.

B. Top off with the cooled syrup and fit the jug with an air lock.

METHOD THREE
USING TAP WATER

A. The two methods outlined above are the best ways to top off at the first and second rackings, especially if the wine seems a bit weak, but you may use tap water if the wine tastes particularly strong.

B. Simply fill the jug to the bottom of the neck with tepid tap water and fit with an air lock.

HOW TO FIT AN AIR LOCK

An air lock is a low-pressure valve especially designed to allow fermentation gas to escape from the wine in the secondary container while preventing air from entering. Variously referred to as a fermentation lock or trap, the air lock consists of a plastic or glass tube mounted on a pierced cork or plastic bung. At some point along the tube (depending on the design), there is generally a well or ball (or two) which the winemaker fills with metabisulfite solution (*see* illustration, page 9). Carbon dioxide gas bubbles up through the solution, which acts as a barrier against air and spoilage bacteria.

STEP ONE
STERILIZING THE AIR LOCK

A. Before you rack your wine, make sure that the air lock you use for your secondary container will fit properly.
Rinse the air lock and immerse its cork or plastic bung in stock metabisulfite solution (*see* How to Sterilize with Metabisulfites, page 80).

B. Pour in enough sterile solution to fill the well or ball about half full. Insert the tubing into the pierced cork or plastic bung. If your air lock is glass, handle with care! These break easily.

STEP TWO
FITTING THE AIR LOCK

Press the air lock and bung into the neck of the secondary

container so that it fits securely. The bottom of the air lock should be at least an inch above the level of the wine.

STEP THREE
CHANGING THE STERILE SOLUTION

The sterile solution in an air lock should be replaced every 3 months or so with fresh sterile solution to prevent contamination of the wine.

THE CANDLE TEST

If you've properly racked your wine at the recommended intervals, it should achieve in time the jewel-like clarity necessary before bottling. Type and ripeness of the fruit, sugar content and racking technique and temperature, all help to determine how quickly this will occur. Good wine takes time but ultimately nearly every wine becomes free of cloudiness, haze, and the surface bubbles that signal continuing fermentation.

To determine whether your wine is ready to bottle, inspect it by performing a Candle Test:

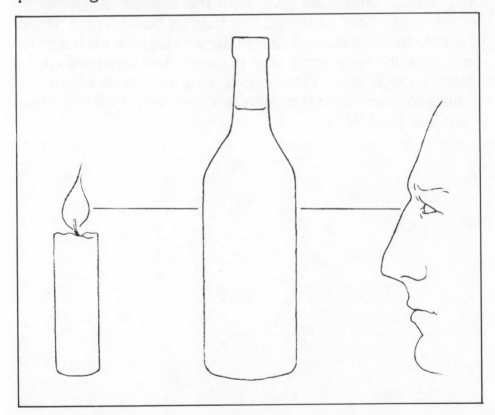

A. Wipe the outside surface of your jug or carboy completely free from dust. Set a lighted candle (or flashlight, if you prefer) a few inches away from the middle of the far side of the jug or carboy.

B. Look through the wine at the flame or light. If the candle flame is sharply outlined and free from distortion and the wine is clear with no floating particles or bubbles on the surface to indicate further fermentation, you may assume that your wine is ready for bottling.

C. Should your wine give *even the slightest* suggestion of cloudiness or haze, or should *any* bubbles be apparent, replace the stale metabisulfite solution in the air lock with fresh solution and allow the wine more time to clear. Most wines will clear if given enough time. However, if wine proves stubborn and refuses to clear within 9 months to a year, fining will sometimes help (*see* page 97).

FINING

The haze or cloudiness that lingers on in a wine that has been given sufficient time to clear is usually due to minute particles in suspension. In this case, fining is the winemaker's last resort. If the wine does not clear within a year after fining, give up and try another wine. You must not bottle cloudy wines.

METHOD ONE
FINING WITH GELATIN

This method will work effectively only if you added grape tannin when preparing the must, or in a red grape wine naturally high in tannin.

A. For each gallon of wine, use ⅛ teaspoon of gelatin. Soften the gelatin in a little water, then heat just until it dissolves. Cool.

B. Stir the cooled gelatin into the wine without disturbing the sediment. Replace the air lock. Allow to stand until clear.

C. If the wine passes the Candle Test, rack into bottles. (Ninety-nine out of a hundred wines do eventually clear.)

METHOD TWO
FINING WITH EGG WHITE

Fining with egg white is more convenient when dealing with at least 10 gallons of wine, but you may also fine smaller quantities by using about 1 teaspoon of beaten egg white for each gallon of wine.

A. For 10 gallons of wine beat 1 egg white to a froth. Mix thoroughly with 3 or 4 cups of the wine. Stir this mixture into the bulk of the wine without disturbing the sediment. Replace the air lock.

B. When the wine passes the Candle Test, rack into bottles.

METHOD THREE
FINING WITH PECTIC ENZYMES

If you've made wine from a stone fruit, that stubborn haze may be due to pectin. In this case use a pectic enzyme to fine.

A. Follow manufacturer's directions regarding the right amount to add.

B. Allow the wine to clear until it passes a Candle Test, then rack into bottles.

HOW TO BOTTLE AND STORE WINES

Although you are probably impatient to bottle your wine (and who can blame you, since the sooner you bottle the wine, the sooner you can drink it), the one rule in winemaking you must not transgress is that bottling should never, ever, be rushed. Good wine takes time—time to undergo secondary fermentation before being racked, and time to develop bouquet and flavor while aging in the bottles.

WHEN TO BOTTLE

Wine should be perfectly clear before bottling, with no suggestion of haze or cloudiness (*see* Candle Test, page 95). If it appears even slightly hazy, the wine needs further aging.

Examine the wine at this time to make sure a heavy deposit of yeast sediment has not formed in the bottom of the jug. Over a period of time a heavy deposit will begin to feed on itself, causing fermentation to begin all over again. If the sediment is more than ⅛-inch deep, rack the wine a fourth time. Fit the jug with an air lock filled with fresh metabisulfite solution and store in a cool, dark place for a month before performing another Candle Test.

HOW TO BOTTLE WINES

STEP ONE
CHECK THE TEMPERATURE OF THE WINE

Bring your wine to about 60 to 65 degrees F. just before bottling.

STEP TWO
ASSEMBLE YOUR EQUIPMENT

For each gallon of wine you will need:

> 5 Standard 25-ounce wine bottles (or 4 standard 25-ounce bottles and 2 half-bottles)
> Appropriate closures
> (Corks are essential for good wines, especially grape wines, but screw-top closures are satisfactory for fruit and flower wines.)
> Siphon hose (to rack the wine into the bottles)
> A corking device to drive in corks

STEP THREE
STERILIZE YOUR EQUIPMENT

See How to Sterilize with Metabisulfites, page 80. Leave a *few* drops of metabisulfite sterilized solution in the bottom of each bottle.

STEP FOUR
RACK WINE INTO BOTTLES

Rack the wine very quietly into the bottles, cutting off the flow as each bottle is filled by pinching the siphon with your fingers just above the bottle neck. This keeps the wine from backing up into the secondary container. Always leave room in the neck of the bottle for the corks.

STEP FIVE
APPLY CLOSURES

A. Always use new wine corks or screw tops.

B. Use a corking device (*see* Sources of Supply, page 107) to drive in corks to proper position below the rim of the bottle.

C. Stand corked bottles upright for 2 or 3 days to allow the corks to dry. Then lay the bottles on their sides.

D. Examine the corks after one week in storage. If any of the bottles is leaking, withdraw the cork and insert another.

E. A professional touch at this point is to seal the corks or caps with foil.

HOW TO STORE WINES

A. Whether a bottle has been corked or capped determines how you store the wine. Screw-top bottles may be stored upright. Corked bottles must be stored on their sides to permit contact of wine and cork to prevent the cork from shrinking. Each corked bottle also needs its own cradle in the rack to keep it from being jostled by its neighbors.

B. The ideal storage temperature for wine should range between 45 degrees F. and 55 degrees F.; however, the important thing to remember is that sudden or frequent temperature change affects wine adversely. Suitable storage is a constantly cool, preferably dark, place where the bottles will not be exposed to vibration or odors.

C. Because wine develops flavor and bouquet in the bottle, it will generally be vastly improved the longer you wait before drinking it. A good rule-of-thumb for deciding when to sample a red grape wine is to age it in the bottle at least as long as it took the wine to clear in the secondary container.

D. If you divide part of your finished wine into half-bottles, you can use these as sample bottles. When you can't contain your curiosity any longer, open a small bottle. If the wine still tastes a bit raw, age the remaining bottles for at least 3 months longer. Continue to sample and age the wine.

E. White grape wine, fruit wines and flower wines generally should not age more than 1 year in the bottle. Exceptions to this rule exist, of course, but don't let your wines age so long that they die in the bottle. When your wine suits your taste buds, drink it. Set one bottle aside, if you like, and let it age for 6 months longer than the other bottles. Taste this wine and make a note of whether it tasted better or worse than the wine did when you first judged it to be mature. Age subsequent batches accordingly.

TROUBLESHOOTING

STUCK FERMENTATIONS

If, during primary fermentation, your daily hydrometer or saccharometer reading remains the same for several days in a row, your must may be suffering from a "stuck" fermentation. Though this "sticking" is usually temporary—the must will generally right itself and begin fermenting again just as suddenly as it stopped—there are several reasons why a must or wine might stop fermenting prematurely.

If your must drops less than one point during the course of a week (even if you don't have a hydrometer or saccharometer you can notice the absence of yeast activity when you stir each day), ask yourself these questions:

1. Did I skimp on yeast nutrient?
2. Have I provided a sufficient amount of acid?
3. Could I have added too much sugar? Or too little?
4. Has the must temperature risen too high or fallen too low?

If you have followed the recipes in this book *exactly,* have properly balanced your ingredients with a hydrometer or saccharometer and have maintained correct temperatures, you should have no trouble. However, if you have not measured your sugar content and suspect that the cause is too little sugar, add a bit of cooled boiled syrup.

A *too heavily* sugared must can also cause trouble. In this case, dilute with water or fruit juice. Sometimes you can unstick a stuck must by vigorous stirring with a longhandled spoon, which aerates it and releases any carbon dioxide gas trapped within. Most musts will respond to these measures, unless incorrect temperatures have caused the sticking.

TEMPERATURE

Proper fermentation temperatures are all-important in wine-making. Musts need to be brought to between 72 and 78 degrees F. before the yeast is added. Temperatures higher than 80 degrees F. may make the wine bitter; at 85 degrees F. the yeast may be seriously weakened.

On the other hand, too cool a temperature can also cause your must to stick as described above. If so, adjust by warming your storage place to the proper fermentation temperature.

BROWNING IN WINES

If the winemaker skips or skimps on the use of pectic enzymes, especially when preparing wines from stone fruits, wines may brown. To avoid spoiling your wines, add pectic enzymes in the amount prescribed in each recipe.

Red wines will brown when overexposed to light or oxygen—always rack, bottle, and store these wines properly.

WINES THAT WILL NOT CLEAR

Occasionally, one wine may stubbornly persist in remaining cloudy. In this case, try fining (*see* Fining, page 97), but bear in mind that this is a last resort. Always give your cloudy wines a chance to clear naturally. Most, given time, will oblige.

GLOSSARY OF WINEMAKING TERMS

Body: The weight of a wine in the mouth. Results mainly from alcohol content and quality of ingredients.

Browning: Occurs when red wines turn brown because of overexposure to light or oxygen or when wines from stone fruits are prepared with too little pectic enzyme.

Carboy: A 5-gallon secondary container.

Cap: The floating layer of fruit pulp which rises to the surface during primary fermentation.

Fining: A process used to clear wines if racking does not eliminate cloudiness.

Lees: The sediment or insoluble matter that settles to the bottom of primary or secondary containers during fermentation.

Must: The combination of fruit, juice, sugar and other ingredients prepared for fermentation. Must does not become wine until it has been racked for the first time.

Primary Fermentation: The first fermentation, characterized by vigorous yeast activity, which is the only step in winemaking that benefits from exposure to the air.

Racking: The process of siphoning, or transferring, wine from one container to another.

Secondary Fermentation: Fermentation from which air is excluded by means of an air lock.

Stone Fruits: Any fruit with a large pit or stone.

TABLE FOR ADJUSTING SUGAR IN THE MUST

SPECIFIC GRAVITY	BALLING	SUGAR IN OUNCES TO BE ADDED PER GALLON TO RAISE MUST ONE POINT
1.000	0	
1.004	1.0	31.5
1.008	2.0	30.0
1.012	3.0	28.5
1.015	4.0	27.0
1.020	5.0	25.5
1.023	6.0	24.0
1.026	7.0	22.5
1.030	8.0	21.0
1.034	9.0	19.5
1.038	10.0	18.0
1.042	11.0	16.5
1.046	12.0	15.0
1.050	13.0	13.5
1.055	14.0	12.0
1.059	15.0	10.5
1.063	16.0	9.0
1.067	17.0	7.5
1.072	18.0	6.0
1.076	19.0	4.5
1.080	20.0	3.0
1.084	21.0	1.5
1.088	22.0	0.0

SOURCES OF SUPPLY

Unless you're fortunate enough to have a local source for wine-making supplies, you'll probably have to write to one of the following for your yeast, acids, etc., plus most of the specialized equipment necessary in winemaking. Send for catalogs from the following companies, all ready and willing to handle individual orders:

Enology Shop, 18 N. Central Avenue, Hartsdale, N.Y. 10530

Milan Laboratories, 57 Spring Street, New York, N.Y.

Presque Isle Wine Cellars, 9440 Buffalo Road, North East, Pa. 16428

Semplex of U.S.A., Box 12276, 4805 Lyndale Avenue North, Minneapolis, Minn. 55412

Wine Art of America, Inc., 4324 Geary Boulevard, San Francisco, Calif. 94118

> Wine Art has many outlets throughout the country and will give you the location of the one nearest you.

Sears, Roebuck & Co., a generally fast and reliable source, lists many winemaking supplies in their catalog.

YVONNE YOUNG TARR is a veteran cookbook writer. Her books include *The Ten Minute Gourmet Cookbook, The Ten Minute Gourmet Diet Cookbook, 101 Desserts to Make You Famous, Love Portions, The New York Times Natural Foods Dieting Book, The Complete Outdoor Cookbook, The New York Times Bread and Soup Cookbook, The Farmhouse Cookbook* and *The Up-with-Wholesome, Down-with-Storebought Book of Recipes and Household Formulas.*
She is married to sculptor William Tarr. They have two children, Jonathon and Nicolas.

NOTES

NOTES

NOTES

NOTES

NOTES

NOTES

NOTES

NOTES

NOTES

NOTES